This Book Belongs To:

Aloha!

Experience the warmth of Hawai'i during your visit to these enchanting islands. We welcome you to the Aloha State and present you with this lei and activity coloring book. Dive into the pages and discover the wonders of Hawai'i!

The Hawaiian Alphabet

There are 12 letters in the Hawaiian alphabet, plus the 'okina ('). Color the letters with crazy patterns!

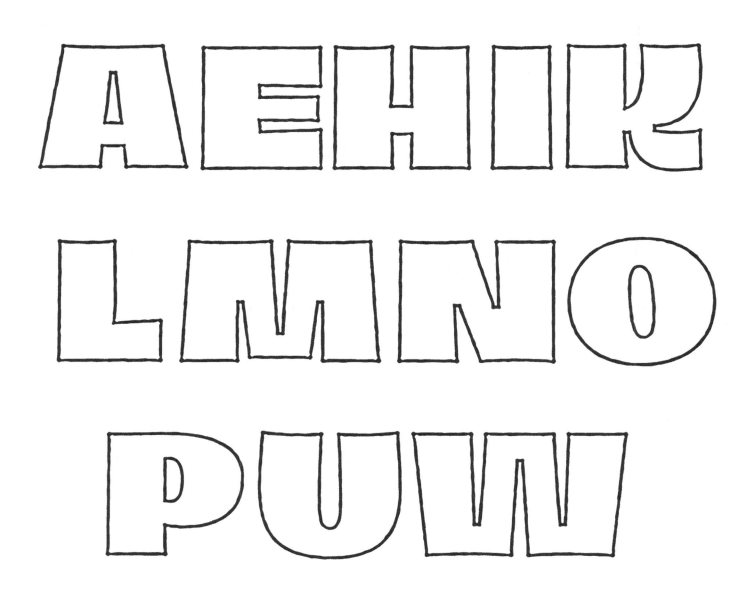

What Is Your Hawaiian Name?

Discover your Hawaiian name. Replace letters in your name with one of the 12 letters from the Hawaiian alphabet.

- Keep the letters in your name that are in the Hawaiian Alphabet, KEEP: A, E, H, I, K, L, M, N, O, P, U & W
- Change B and F to **P**
- Change C, D, G, J, Q, S, T, X, and Z to **K**
- Change R to **L**
- Change V to **W**
- Change Y to **I**
- Remember to separate all consonants with a vowel of your choosing

Examples: JEREMY = KELEMI, CATHERINE = KAKOHELINE

WRITE YOUR HAWAIIAN NAME IN THE TAG BELOW

HELLO
MY NAME IS

WORDS & PHRASES TO KNOW BEFORE YOU GO

Find the common Hawaiian words & phrases in the word search

 Aloha = Love, hello, or goodbye

 Mahalo = Thank you

 Lanai = Patio or balcony

 Kama'aina = Local person from Hawaii

 Ohana = Family

 No Ka 'Oi = The Best

 Wahine = Woman

 Ono = Delicious

 'A Hui Hou = Until we meet again

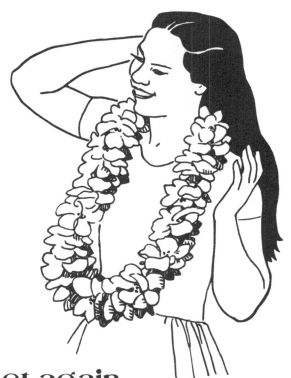

Hawaiian and English are the official languages of Hawaii.
Fun Fact: It is the only state in America with 2 official languages.

```
E R W A N O U H R D G B W S R Y
A Z N G F R N W W O I A N A L Y
K H F A R D E D N I E T O H J Y
A Y T Z T X W Y W U F N H L F X
D Y I R O A X A H U I H O U Z U
B Q X R J F E S O A Q Q B I Y E
N A N A H O Q U L S X J M A T O
O C H K Y S I O D U A O L E X T
N L G E E L H O E R N L J L J Z
O Q M N R A N L T A I A Q N U T
K E L I T S R Q B L A H Q H L H
A O N H N R E L I H A A N U H U
O B F A V O H V J N M M C E R E
I M N W N U C O Z O A X C L Q N
M C X O D F H D W Z K L S W B E
U T C M T I F R U P G I W G N Y
```

A HUI HOU	ALOHA
KAMAAINA	LANAI
MAHALO	NO KA OI
OHANA	ONO
WAHINE	

WORDS & PHRASES
TO KNOW BEFORE YOU GO

Find the common Hawaiian words & phrases in the word search

 Mauka = Mountain

 Makai = Ocean

 Howzit? = Slang for "How Are You?"

 Keiki - Child

 Ohana = Family

 Pupu = Appetizer

 Honu = Sea turtle

 E Como Mai = Welcome

 Kane = Man

The Hawaiian alphabet consists of 12 letters, with 5 vowels and 7 consonants.
Fun Fact: Hawaiian words always end with a vowel

```
G G M K E J M E K D C F Y J Q E
O W G N N Z P Z M N M A K A I Z
D Y Q U Q T H I V H X C V I P S
O Z J B N Q X O F M Q X K U X O
I G B P U O T D Q E P U U M F S
Q P M Q H B H F T U J Y W G Z D
K S X S J W P B P W Z K M F D A
M D I M I I M U B M S B W O N H
I S Z A S L J P Z X A K E I K I
F V Q K M C W R W G E G U D N H
N M W I A O T M O M A U K A G T
W F U P H N M B U W R P R Z I A
Y O A G V U E O V U P B Q Z S X
F F P O H A N A C P S M W O A I
I H E U W I K S O E D O O X Y H
L R E F F S V O N D H Z Z X C V
```

E COMO MAI	HONU
HOWZIT	KANE
KEIKI	MAKAI
MAUKA	OHANA
PUPU	

Flag of Hawai'i

Hawai'i became the 50th state of the United States of America on August 21, 1959.

Color the state flag of Hawai'i using the number & color guide below.

Fun Fact: Hawai's flag is the only U.S. state flag to have a foreign country's national flag represented on it. Do you know which country's flag it is?

State Bird

DRAW THE NENE

State Fish
Color the
Humuhumunukunukuapua'a

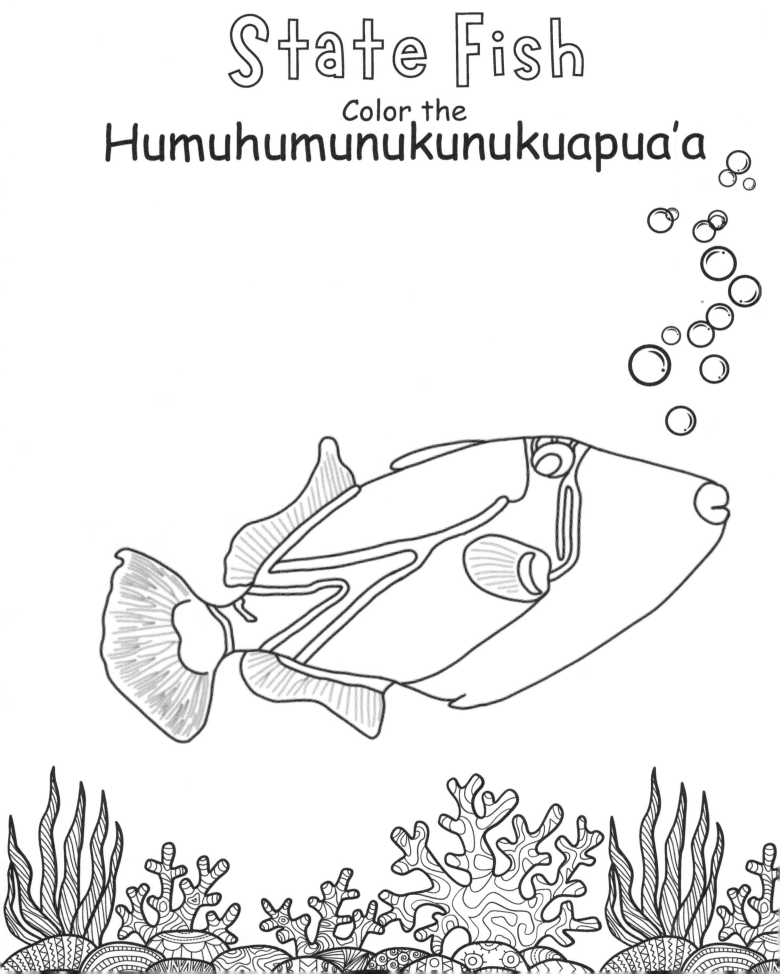

There are 21 letters in the name of the state fish. How many words can you create using the letters in humuhumunukunukuapua'a?

_____   _____

_____   _____

_____   _____

_____   _____

_____   _____

_____   _____

_____   _____

State Flower

Color the
Yellow Hibiscus

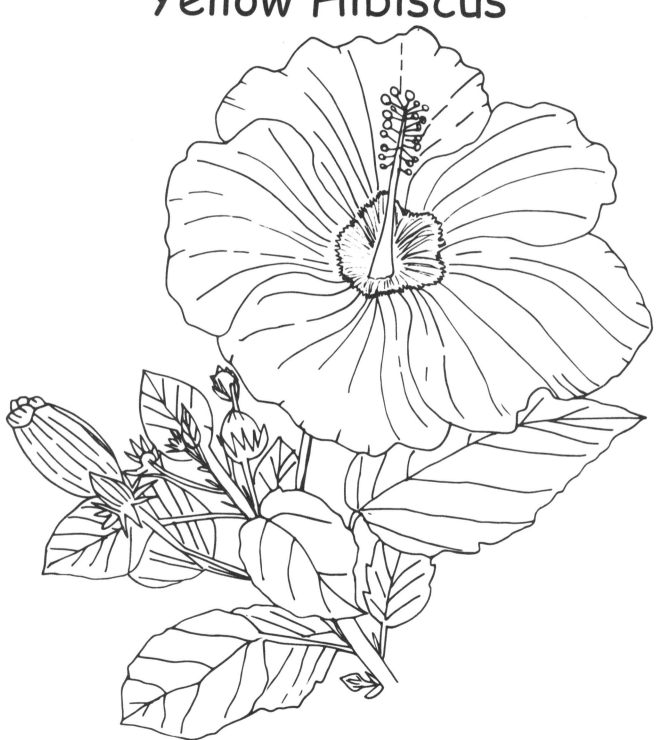

The Hawaiian Islands

Hawai'i is an archipelago made up of 8 main islands, several atolls & many islets.

Color the island(s) you are visiting on your trip.

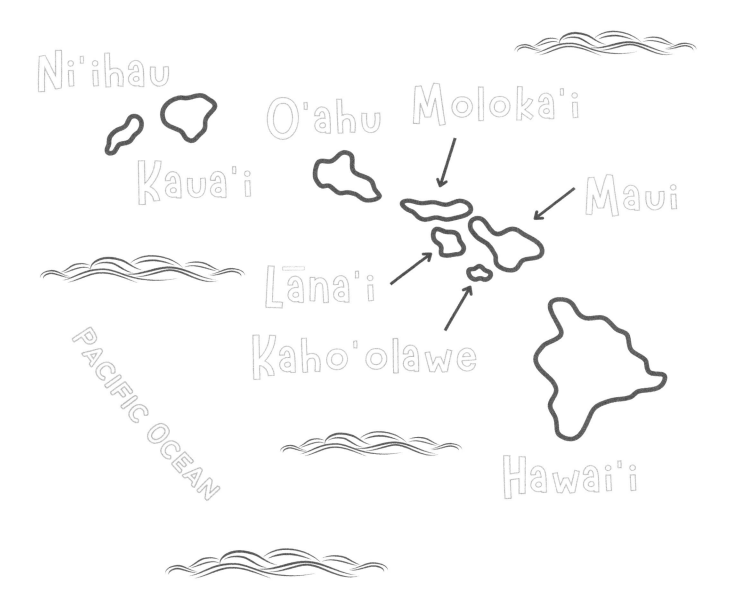

Fun Fact: You will definitely NOT be visiting Kaho'olawe or Ni'ihau as they are not open to the general public.

Fun Island Facts: Hawai'i

Connect the dots to see the shape of the islands.
Color the official island flowers of each island.

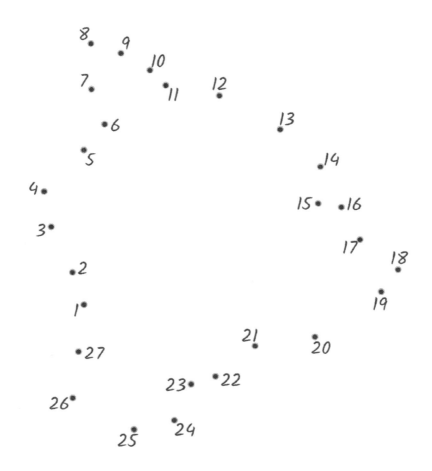

The Island of Hawai'i is the largest island in the United States at over 4,000 square miles.

Nickname: The Big Island

Places of Interest: Hawai'i Volcanoes National Park, Mauna Kea, Akaka Falls, Hawai'i Tropical Botanical Garden, Kona & Hilo

Population: 200,629

Fun Island Facts: Hawai'i

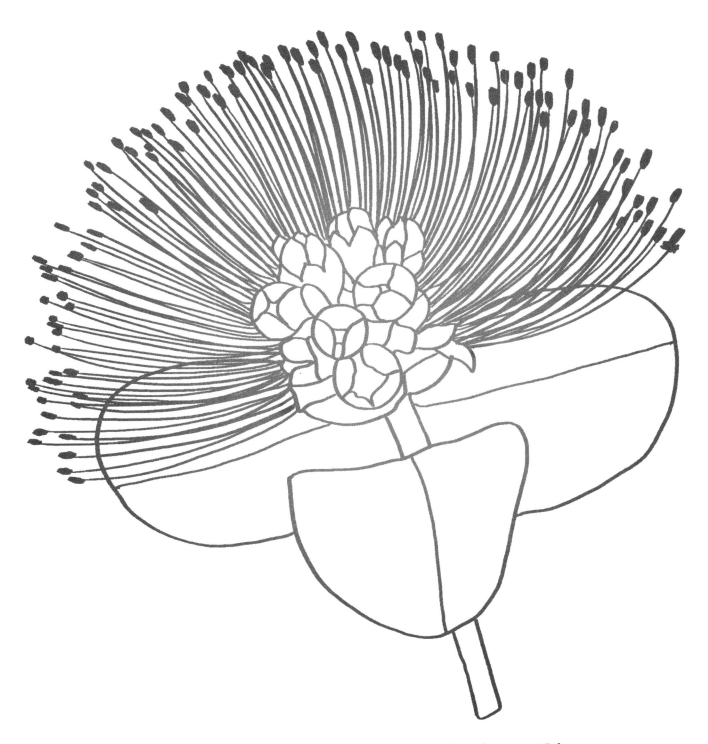

Official Flower of Hawai'i - Lehua Flower
Official Island Color - Red

Fun Island Facts: Maui

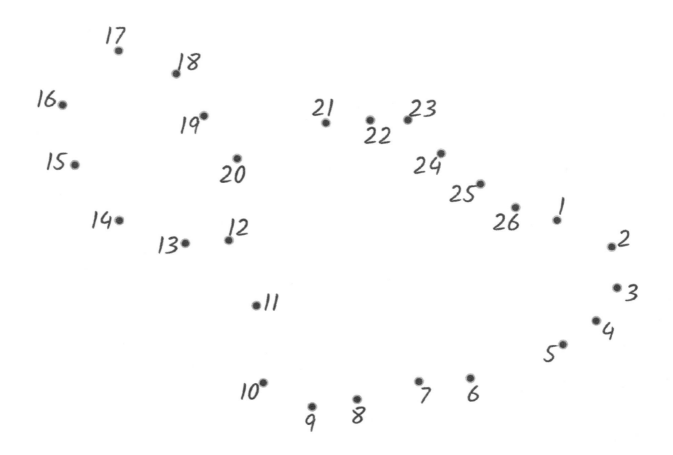

Maui is the 2nd largest island and is divided by two mountain ranges—Haleakala and West Maui Mountains.

Nickname: The Valley Isle

Places of Interest: Haleakala National Park, Lahaina, Road to Hana, Napili Beach, Ho'okipa Beach Park & Molokini Crater

Population: 168,307

Fun Island Facts: Maui

Official Flower of Maui - Lokelani Rose
Official Island Color - Pink

Fun Island Facts: O'ahu

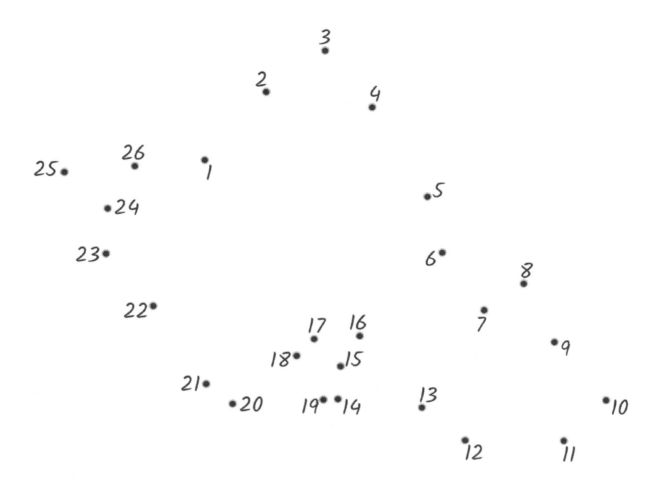

O'ahu has the highest population count in the state. O'ahu is home to the city of Honolulu, which is the state's capital.

Nickname: The Gathering Place

Places of Interest: Diamond Head, The North Shore, USS Arizona Memorial at Pearl Harbor, Waikiki, Hanauma Bay, and Ko Olina.

Population: 1,016,508

Fun Island Facts: O'ahu

Official Flower of O'ahu - Ilima Flower
Official Island Color - Yellow

Fun Island Facts: Kaua'i

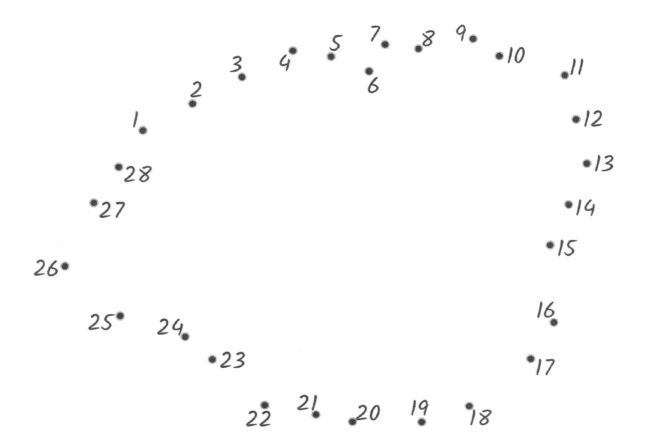

Kaua'i is the oldest of the Hawaiian islands at about 5.1 millions years old. Kaua'i is known for it's beautiful and lush scenery, with valleys & jungles.

Nickname: The Garden Isle

Places of Interest: Waimea Canyon, Na Pali Coast State Park, Kalalau Beach, Wailua River and Hanalei.

Population: 73, 298

Fun Island Facts: Kaua'i

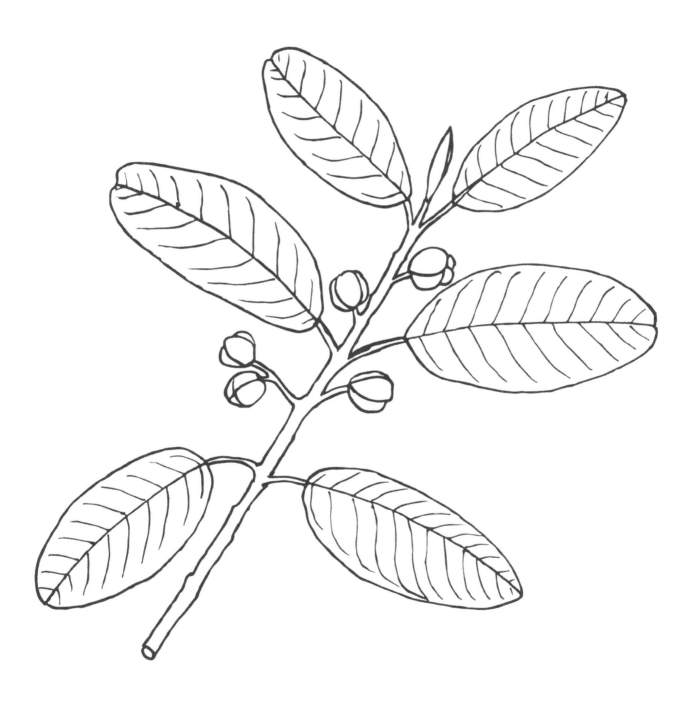

Official Flower of Kaua'i - Mokihana Berry
Official Island Color - Purple

Fun Island Facts: Moloka'i

1. 2.
3. 4. 5. 6. 8. 9.
27
26.
7 10 11 12 13 14
22
25.
24 23 21 19 16
20 18 17 15

 Moloka'i has the largest percentage of native Hawaiians and is believed to be the place where the hula began.

Nickname: The Friendly Isle

Places of Interest: Kalaupapa National Historical Park, Kaunakakai Harbor & Kapuaiwa Coconut Grove.

Population: 7,345

Fun Island Facts: Moloka'i

Official Flower of Moloka'i - Pua Kukui
Official Island Color - Green

Fun Island Facts: Lāna'i

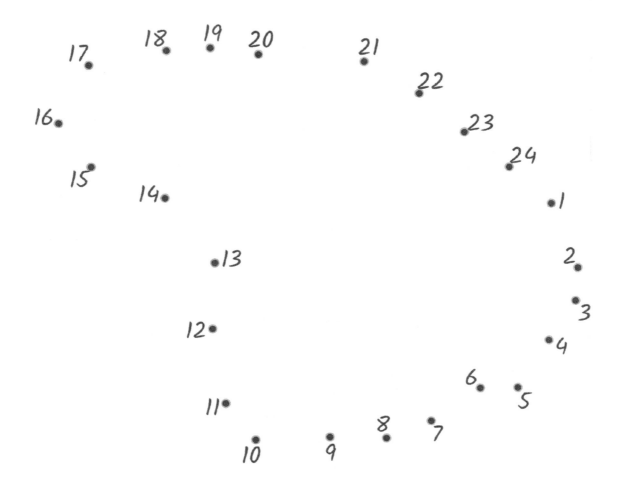

Lāna'i is the sixth largest island and it once produced 75 percent of the world's exported pineapples.

Nickname: The Pineapple Isle

Places of Interest: Lāna'i City, Hulopoe Beach, Ship Wreck Beach, Keahiakawelo & Polihua Beach

Population: 3,367

Fun Island Facts: Lāna'i

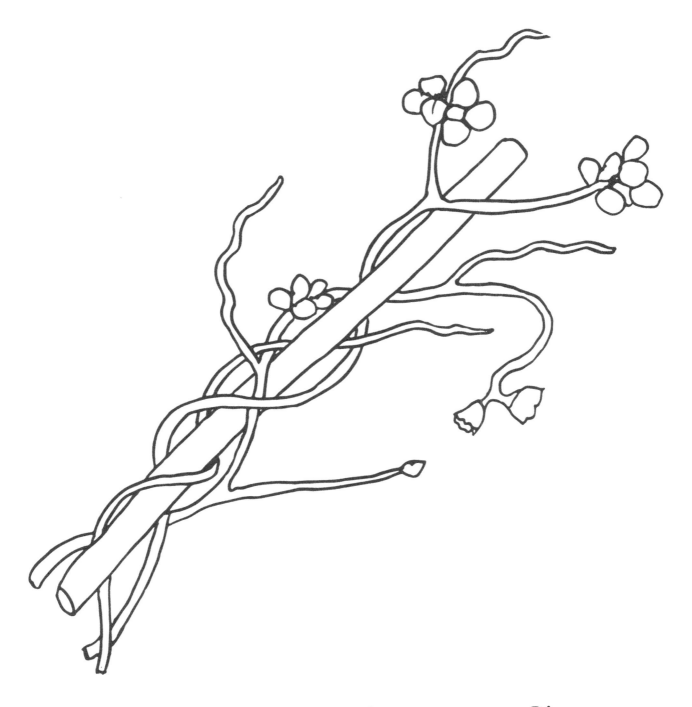

Official Flower of Lāna'i - Kaunaoa Plant
Official Island Color - Orange

Fun Island Facts: Ni'ihau

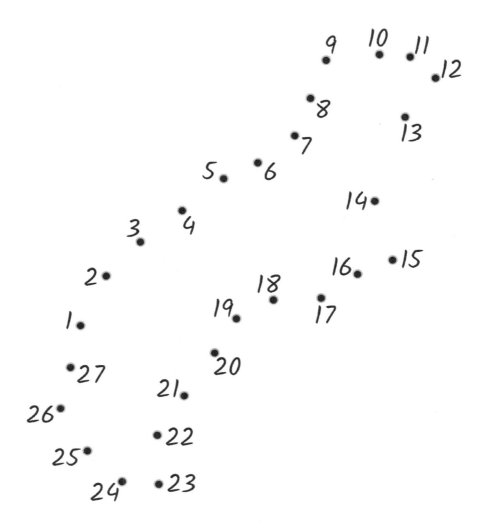

Ni'ihau has been owned by the Robinson Family since 1864 and it is the only island where Hawaiian is spoken as the primary language.

Nickname: The Forbidden Isle, as visitors are not permitted unless invited by the Robinson Family.

Population: 84

Fun Island Facts: Ni'ihau

Official "Flower" of Ni'ihau - White pupu shells
Official Island Color - White

Fun Island Facts: Kaho'olawe

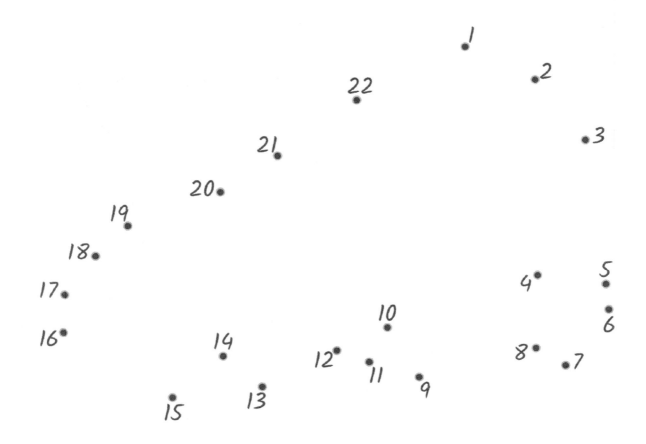

Kaho'olawe is the smallest island and was used by the United States military during World War II. Today the island is still prohibited to the public.

Nickname: The Target Isle

Population: 0

Fun Island Facts: Kaho'olawe

Official Flower of Kaho'olawe - Hinahina plant
Official Island Color - Gray

Nickname Match

Match the island to its nickname.

Lana'i	The Friendly Isle
Hawai'i	The Big Island
Moloka'i	The Forbidden Isle
O'ahu	The Valley Isle
Maui	The Garden Isle
Ni'ihau	The Target Isle
Kaua'i	The Pineapple Isle
Kaho'olawe	The Gathering Place

Food Bucket List

Try these Hawaiian foods and rate them.
(Remember ono means delicious)

Shave Ice

Location: _____

Cost: _____

Notes: _____

_____

_____

_____

How ono is it? ☆☆☆☆☆

Loco Moco

Location: _____

Cost: _____

Notes: _____

_____

_____

_____

How ono is it? ☆☆☆☆☆

Poi

Location: _____

Cost: _____

Notes: _____

_____

_____

_____

How ono is it? ☆☆☆☆☆

Laulau

Location: _____

Cost: _____

Notes: _____

_____

_____

_____

How ono is it? ☆☆☆☆☆

Malasada

Location: --

Cost: --

Notes: --

How ono is it?   ☆☆☆☆☆

Manapua

Location: --

Cost: --

Notes: --

How ono is it?   ☆☆☆☆☆

Spam Musubi

Location: _____

Cost: _____

Notes: _____

_____

_____

_____

How ono is it? ☆☆☆☆☆

Saimin

Location: _____

Cost: _____

Notes: _____

_____

_____

_____

How ono is it? ☆☆☆☆☆

Hawai'i Bucket List

Check off this list when completed.
Add more adventures to your must-do list!

- [ ] Snorkeling
- [ ] Beach Trips
- [ ] Surf Lessons
- [ ] Hiking
- [ ] Visit Zippy's
- [ ] Go to a Luau
- [ ] _____
- [ ] _____
- [ ] _____
- [ ] _____
- [ ] _____
- [ ] _____
- [ ] _____
- [ ] _____

Musical Instruments of Hawai'i

Color the instruments.

Ipu

The ipu is a percussion instrument that is made from gourds grown on the islands.

The ukulele was brought to Hawai'i by Portugese immigrants.

Ukulele

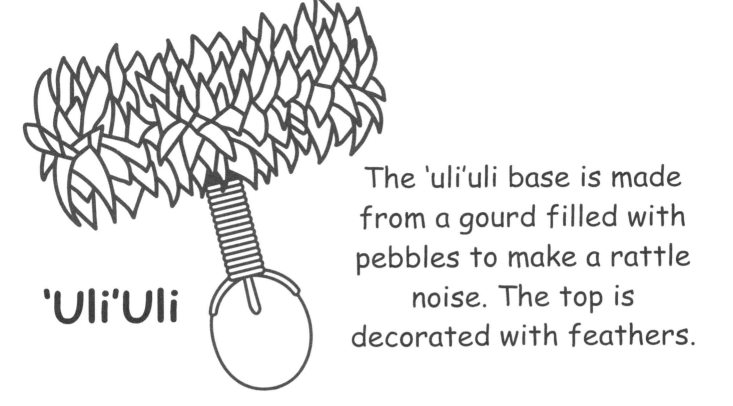

'Uli'Uli

The 'uli'uli base is made from a gourd filled with pebbles to make a rattle noise. The top is decorated with feathers.

The pahu is carved from one piece of wood. It is used during hula performances and other cultural ceremonies.

Pahu

Hula - Basic Steps

Hula is a Hawaiian dance expressing a chant or song. Learn some basic steps.

Take two steps to the side then two steps back the other way.

Kāholo

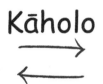

Sway your hips side to side.

Ka'ō

Heal taps the floor and toes stay on ground. The other foot steps forward then back for 1-2 repetitions. Repeat with the opposite feet.

Kāwelu

Keep knees bent with weight on one hip, with the opposite foot & leg extended at a 45 degree angle from the body.

Hela

Rotate hips in a circular motion.

'Ami

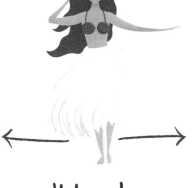

'Uwehe

Lift one foot up and when it touches the ground, both heels lift, pushing the knees forward and to the side, while the hips sway, then both feet touch the ground. Repeat with the opposite foot.

String a Lei Game Rules

Have fun with this version of the classic game Hangman.

Setup: One player thinks of a word and marks blanks for each letter in the word box. The other player tries to guess the word by suggesting letters.

Guessing: The guessing player suggests a letter. If the letter is in the word, the other player fills in the blanks with that letter. If not, you draw a line from one flower to the next, starting with flower 1.

Number of Incorrect Guesses: There's a limit of 7 incorrect guesses. If the lei is fully strung, connecting all 7 flowers, before the word is guessed, the guessing player loses.

Winning/Losing: The guessing player wins by guessing the word before the lei is fully strung. If the lei is complete before guessing the word, the player who thought of the word wins.

String a Lei

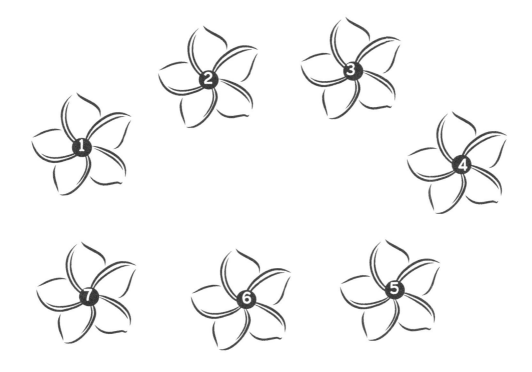

WORD: ....

A B C D E F G H I J K L M
N O P Q R S T U V W X Y Z

THE WINNER: ....

String a Lei

WORD: ....

A B C D E F G H I J K L M
N O P Q R S T U V W X Y Z

THE WINNER: ....

String a Lei

WORD: ....

A B C D E F G H I J K L M
N O P Q R S T U V W X Y Z

THE WINNER: ....

String a Lei

WORD: ....

A B C D E F G H I J K L M
N O P Q R S T U V W X Y Z

THE WINNER: ....

String a Lei

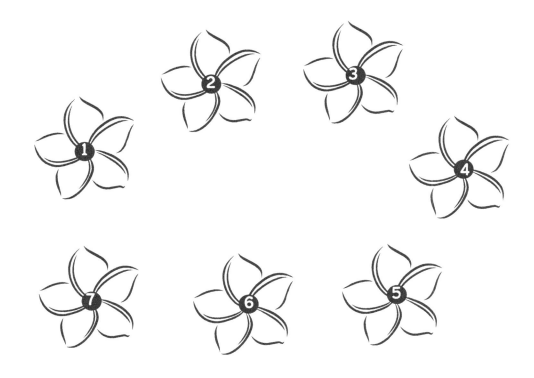

WORD: ....

A B C D E F G H I J K L M
N O P Q R S T U V W X Y Z

THE WINNER: ....

String a Lei

WORD: ....

A B C D E F G H I J K L M
N O P Q R S T U V W X Y Z

THE WINNER: ....

String a Lei

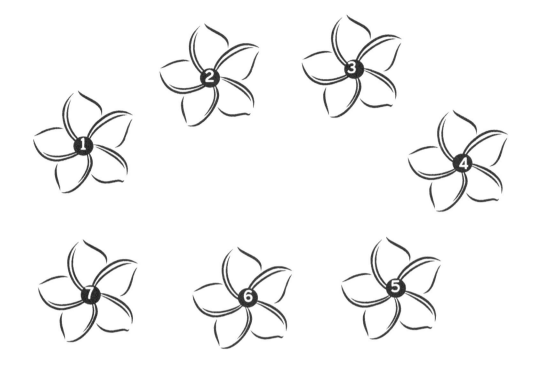

WORD: ....

A B C D E F G H I J K L M
N O P Q R S T U V W X Y Z

THE WINNER: ....

Color Your Hawaiian Shirt

FUN FACT: Every Friday is 'Aloha Friday' in Hawai'i. You'll find business people in their aloha shirts and attire.

Decorate your Hawaiian Shirt

Hawaiian shirts are colorful, fun, and have a tropical theme/print.
Have fun decorating your shirt!

TIC TAC TOE

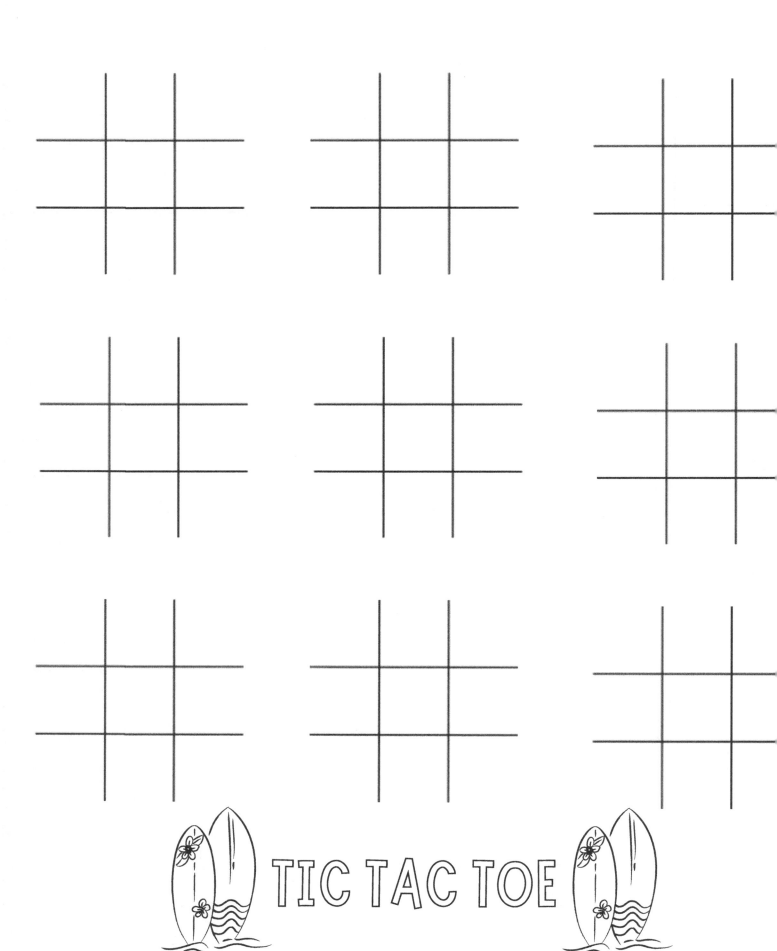

TIC TAC TOE

TIC TAC TOE

Dots & Boxes

Game Rules
1. Players take turns drawing lines between two adjacent dots.
2. If a player completes the fourth side of a box, they write their initial in the box and take another turn.
3. The game continues until no more lines can be drawn.
4. The player with the most captured boxes at the end of the game wins.

Dots & Boxes

Player 1 # of Boxes =
Player 2 # of Boxes =

Winner_____

Dots & Boxes

Player 1 # of Boxes =
Player 2 # of Boxes =

Winner_____

Dots & Boxes

Player 1 # of Boxes =
Player 2 # of Boxes =

Winner_____

Hawai'i Travel Journal

TRAVEL JOURNAL

Date:

Today I visited...

I really enjoyed...

Something new I learned is...

Im looking forward to...

Notes:

TRAVEL JOURNAL

Date:

Today I visited... _____

_____

I really enjoyed... _____

_____

Something new I learned is... _____

_____

Im looking forward to... _____

_____

Notes: _____

_____

_____

_____

TRAVEL JOURNAL

Date:

Today I visited... _____

_____

I really enjoyed... _____

_____

Something new I learned is... _____

_____

I'm looking forward to... _____

_____

Notes: _____

_____

_____

_____

TRAVEL JOURNAL

Date:

Today I visited...

I really enjoyed...

Something new I learned is...

I'm looking forward to...

Notes:

TRAVEL JOURNAL

Date:

Today I visited... _____

_____

I really enjoyed... _____

_____

Something new I learned is... _____

_____

Im looking forward to... _____

_____

Notes: _____

_____

_____

_____

TRAVEL JOURNAL

Date:

Today I visited... _____

_____

I really enjoyed... _____

_____

Something new I learned is... _____

_____

I'm looking forward to... _____

_____

Notes: _____
_____
_____
_____

TRAVEL JOURNAL

Date:

Today I visited... _____

_____

I really enjoyed... _____

Something new I learned is... _____

Im looking forward to... _____

Notes: _____

_____

_____

_____

TRAVEL JOURNAL

Date:

Today I visited... _____

_____

I really enjoyed... _____

_____

Something new I learned is... _____

_____

I'm looking forward to... _____

_____

Notes: _____

_____

_____

_____

TRAVEL JOURNAL

Date:

Today I visited... _____

I really enjoyed... _____

Something new I learned is... _____

Im looking forward to... _____

Notes: _____
_____
_____
_____

TRAVEL JOURNAL

Date:

Today I visited... _____

I really enjoyed... _____

Something new I learned is... _____

Im looking forward to... _____

Notes: _____
_____
_____
_____

TRAVEL JOURNAL

Date:

Today I visited... _____

_____

I really enjoyed... _____

_____

Something new I learned is... _____

_____

Im looking forward to... _____

_____

Notes: _____

_____

_____

_____

TRAVEL JOURNAL

Date:

Today I visited... _____

I really enjoyed... _____

Something new I learned is... _____

Im looking forward to... _____

Notes: _____
_____
_____
_____

TRAVEL JOURNAL

Date:

Today I visited... _____

I really enjoyed... _____

Something new I learned is... _____

Im looking forward to... _____

Notes: _____
_____
_____
_____

TRAVEL JOURNAL

Date:

Today I visited...

I really enjoyed...

Something new I learned is...

I'm looking forward to...

Notes:

TRAVEL JOURNAL

Date:

Today I visited... _____

I really enjoyed... _____

Something new I learned is... _____

I'm looking forward to... _____

Notes: _____
_____
_____
_____

Mahalo for Visiting
&
'A Hui Ho...

Made in the USA
Las Vegas, NV
10 June 2024